S0-CBP-403

The Jelling Stone was erected about
980 A.D. by King Harald Bluetooth and
inscribed in memory of his parents, King
Gorm the Old and Queen Thyra. (Gorm
united Jutland and nearby islands into
a Denmark resembling today's borders.)
This early writing, called runes, is the
inspiration for the headlines in this book.

DANISH PROVERBS

Compiled by
Julie Jensen McDonald
Editing, Calligraphy and
Illustration by
Esther Feske

Penfield
Press

Books by mail, each $8.95 postpaid:
        Danish Proverbs
        Finnish Proverbs
        German Proverbs
        Scottish Proverbs
        Scandinavian Proverbs
1993 prices, subject to change.
For a list of all ethnic titles, write:
        Penfield Press
        215 Brown Street
        Iowa City, Iowa 52245

Remains of numerous Viking ships have been found in northern Europe. The Viking Ship Museum in Roskilde displays several of these 1,000-year-old relics. Built mostly of oak, these light and seaworthy open vessels were powered by a large square sail and rows of oarsmen.

THE AUTHOR

Julie Jensen McDonald, whose ancestry is Danish, was born in a western Iowa Danish community. She is noted for an immigrant novel with Danish roots, Amalie. For Penfield Press, she has authored Delectably Danish Recipes and Reflections, Scandinavian Proverbs, and Definitely Danish: Denmark and Danish Americans. She served as chair of the Iowa Arts Council, teaches journalism at St. Ambrose University, and is a trustee of the Davenport Museum of Art.

THE ARTIST

Esther Feske, prize-winning graphic designer and calligrapher, has produced four previous books of proverbs for Penfield Press. She received an MFA in graphic design from the University of Iowa and has designed for Penfield's owners since 1974. She was recently president of Escribiente Calligraphic Society in Albuquerque, New Mexico.

1

Front Cover: The Little Mermaid is one of Hans Christian Andersen's most popular fairy-tale characters. Immortalized in bronze by sculptor Edvard Eriksen, she has become the symbol of Copenhagen, where she sits on a rock overlooking the harbor.

Back Cover: Replicas of graceful, fast and strong Viking ships are today enjoyed by tourists. Centuries ago, however, these ships terrorized Europe. Some Scandinavian kings commanded over a thousand ships in staging raids that risked little but returned with treasure, goods and slaves.

The proverbs in this book are principally from A Polyglot of Foreign Proverbs by Henry G. Bohn, Bell & Daldy, 6 York Street, Covent Garden, and 186 Fleet Street, London, 1867.

INTRODUCTION

Webster defines a proverb as "an oft-repeated, pithy and ingeniously turned maxim." A simpler and better definition is "a short, wise saying used for a long time by many people."

Danish proverbs demonstrate the deep practicality, the bedrock optimism, and the sometimes sardonic sense of humor of the national character.

The folk wisdom packaged in a proverb is handed down through many generations, and these short, bright sayings become words to live by.

"My grandmother used to say" prefaces many of the following proverbs in my mind. May you also find what your "grandmother used to say" and more.

Julie Jensen McDonald

3

Ancient Viking burial grounds contrast with modern cities.

SAGE OBSERVATIONS

Beauty without goodness
   is like a rose without fragrance.

Unwilling service earns no thanks.

Who cheats oneself
     is cheated in the worst way.

Do not put in more warp
      than you can weave.

The distance is great
    between saying and doing.

None so deaf as those who won't hear.

Whoever lies down with dogs
    will get up with fleas.

5

Large model ships are often suspended inside churches, representing the importance of the sea and ships to this island nation.

A thief thinks every man steals.

It is easy to manage
when fortune favors.

It is difficult to get many heads
under one hat.

Speech is oft repented,
silence seldom.

He who would serve everybody
gets thanks from nobody.

Advice after action
is like rain after harvest.

Good corn is not reaped
from a bad field.

The Faroe Islands are stark and remote.

Whoever has health
is young enough,
whoever has no debts
is rich enough.

He who controls his tongue
loses least in a quarrel.

The branch that bends
is better than the branch
that breaks.

To hide the truth is to bury gold.

Faint praise is a kind of abuse.

A fool laughs with the crowd
without knowing why.

9

Low rolling hills are a typical landscape.

What no one can take from you,
   you may call your own.

A willing helper does not wait
   to be asked.

Those who will not take
   cheap advice
      will have to buy
         dear repentance.

This round tower and observatory were built by Christian IV in 1642 for the famous astronomer Tycho Brahe.

EXPERIENCE SPEAKS

Giving advice to a fool
        is like throwing water
            on a goose.

A wound never heals so well
        that it leaves no scar.

Whoever would enjoy the fire
        must endure the smoke.

A bold attempt is half the battle.

What is learned painfully
        is remembered long.

He must stand high
        who would see the end
            of his own destiny.

White churches with stepped gables and red tile roofs are a charming sight.

What the snow conceals,
    the thaw reveals.

There is no virtue in a promise
    unless it is kept.

Gold is proved in the fire,
    friendship in need.

You cannot shear sheep
    closer than the skin.

Opportunity makes the thief.

Sow little, reap little.

We must sow,
    even after a bad harvest.

Neatly stacked wood for winter fires.

WORLDLY GOODS

Riches may be abused,
but they are never refused.

The one who can't get bacon
must be content with cabbage.

Honest men do not grow rich
in a hurry.

Luck is better than money.

One who is fed by another's hand
seldom gets enough.

A rich widow's tears are soon dried.

The poor man wants much,
the miser everything.

17

The seaweed-thatched roof of this old farmhouse hosts native wildflowers.

HEARTH & HOME

The pot boils best
on one's own hearth.

A hearth of your own
is worth gold.

You must bake
with the flour you have.

An unpleasant guest is as welcome
as salt to a sore eye.

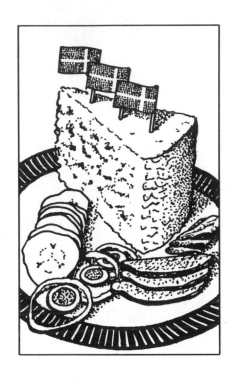

Danes love the Dannebrog, oldest flag
of any European nation, their famous
blue-veined cheese, and smørrebrød,
open-faced sandwiches you assemble
yourself.

EATING & DRINKING

It's a poor roast
      that yields no drippings.

The poor man seeks food,
      the rich man appetite.

The beer goes in
      and the wits go out.

Truth and folly
      dwell in the wine cask.

The stories of Hans Christian Andersen,
perhaps the most famous Dane of all,
have been translated into more than 100
languages.

CHILDREN

Correction is good
   when administered in time.

A child's woe is short-lived.

Children are the riches of the poor.

From children you must expect
          childish acts.

A pet child has many names.

Bend the willow when it is young.

A lazy boy and a warm bed
     are hard to separate.

The tiny birthplace of Hans Christian
Andersen, in Odense, is now a museum.

HEART & SOUL

The one who has fewest wants
      is nearest to God.

That which is unsaid may be spoken,
   but the spoken can't be unsaid.

Late to church
      is better than never.

It takes a high wall
      to keep out fear.

A light spirit is needed
      when one's fate is heavy.

Evil tongues and evil ears
         are equally bad.

25

Odense proudly displays the silhouette
of its favorite son.

When anger blinds the eyes,
          truth disappears.

Cheerfulness and good will
          make labor light.

When the wound is healed,
          the pain is forgotten.

Enough is great riches.

Kind words don't wear out
          the tongue.

A golden key opens all doors
          but heaven's.

Hans Christian Andersen was proficient at paper-cutting as well as story-telling.

It is a great art to laugh
at your own misfortunes.

Whoever despises small things
seldom grows rich.

The one who is scared by words
has no heart for deeds.

Folk dancers in national costumes carry on beloved traditions.

FRIENDS & NEIGHBORS

Distrust poisons a friendship.

Old friends and old ways
      should not be scorned.

An open enemy
      is better than a false friend.

Control your mouth
      and keep your friend.

A good neighbor is better than
      a distant brother.

No one is rich enough
      to do without neighbors.

A friend's faults may be noticed,
      but not blamed.

Kronborg Castle was built to defend the Sound at Elsinore, entry to the Baltic Sea. It is the setting for Shakespeare's <u>Hamlet</u>.

WAR & PEACE

Better a pittance in peace
than plenty in strife.

Peace feeds, war wastes;
peace breeds, war consumes.

Peace must be bought
even at a high price.

Peace and a well-built house
cannot be bought too dearly.

Where there is discipline,
there is virtue;
where there is peace,
there is plenty.

Every wind attacks a leaky ship.

A statue in Copenhagen honors Bishop
Absalon, 12th century leader who
ordered that Danish history, laws, myths
and folklore be written down.

LAW & GOVERNMENT

A meager compromise
is better than a fat lawsuit.

B etter no law than law not enforced.

V irtue in the middle, said the Devil,
when seated between two lawyers.

T o circumstances and custom
the law must yield.

H e who would not go to hell
must not go to court.

L awyers and painters
can soon change black to white.

N ecessity knows no law.

35

Frederiksborg Castle in Copenhagen is now the National History Museum.

A silent man's words
are not brought into court.

Justice oft leans to the side
where the purse pulls.

At court they sell a good deal
of smoke without fire.

To obey the law
and to do right
are not always the same.

Money is more eloquent
than a dozen members
of parliament.

Storks are protected and appreciated.

ANIMAL OBSERVATIONS

A crow is never whiter
        for often washing.

The slow cow gets the sour grass.

Though a donkey carries
        a sack of gold,
            it still eats thistles.

Every little bit helps, said the sow
        as she snapped at a gnat.

If the hen did not cackle
        no one would know
        what she had been about.

It is not for the swan
        to teach eaglets to fly.

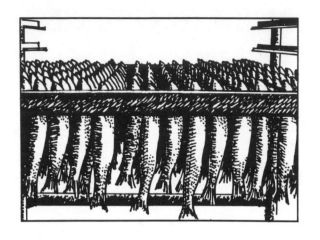

Denmark is noted for its smoked herring.

The piglet must often suffer
for what the old sow did.

Even clever hens
sometimes lay their eggs
among nettles.

When the goose trusts the fox,
then woe to her neck.

We are all well placed, said the cat,
when she was seated
on the bacon.

Guards parade at the Amalienborg
Royal Palace in Copenhagen.

WISE ADVICE

When the game is at its peak,
      it's time to quit.

Honor the tree that shelters you.

Let every bird sing its own note.

Praise a fool,
      and you make him useful.

If you cannot get the bird,
      get one of its feathers.

It is better to ask directions twice
than to lose your way once.

Windmills were used to take advantage
of the breezes that sweep across Denmark.

WRY COMMENTS

Who feeds the hen
      ought to have the egg.

It is poor comfort
      for one who has broken
      his leg
that another has broken his neck.

Every fool thinks he is
      clever enough.

He who tickles himself
      can laugh when he pleases.

A dog is a dog, whatever its color.

No is a good answer
      when given in time.

Danes are never far from water.

Not all who blow the horn
are hunters.

You'll keep your mouth open
a long time
before a roast pigeon flies in.

Better cheap clothes
than bare skin.

There's an end to everything —
except sausage, which has two.

When everyone
minds their own business,
the work gets done.

Better in one piece
than patched with gold.

Iron crosses stand near ancient inscribed stones in the church cemetery at Jelling.

Three women and a goose
　　　　make a market.

When brains fail, luck helps.

Everything has a remedy –
　　　　　　except death.

Woven paper hearts are a traditional Christmas decoration.